Edward Alfred Pollard

The Southern Spy

Letters on the policy and inauguration of the Lincoln war

Edward Alfred Pollard

The Southern Spy
Letters on the policy and inauguration of the Lincoln war

ISBN/EAN: 9783337298401

Printed in Europe, USA, Canada, Australia, Japan

Cover: Foto ©ninafisch / pixelio.de

More available books at **www.hansebooks.com**

THE SOUTHERN SPY.

Letters on the Policy and Inauguration of the Lincoln War.

WRITTEN ANONYMOUSLY IN WASHINGTON AND ELSEWHERE.

By EDWARD A. POLLARD, of Virginia.

Author of "Black Diamonds."

"Justum et tenacem propositi virum,
Non civium ardor prava jubentium,
Non vultus instantis tyranni,
Mente quatit solidâ."—HORACE.

RICHMOND, VA.
WEST & JOHNSTON:
145 MAIN STREET.
1861.

PREFATORY.

The author of these letters, once a Union man, as long as there was a prospect of acquiring and maintaining the constitutional rights of the South in the Union, and of realizing a hope of Christian peace and charity therein; once averse, on politic grounds, to the early movements of secession, as offering a violent resource for what he then hoped might be moderately remedied, sees that Union now affected to be maintained by a despotism, and the former issue of secession now converted into one where the right of self-government is on one side, and a war of despotism, usurped powers, compulsory purposes and wanton atrocities is on the other.

In the essential alteration of the issue, he can only be for the independence of the South, when it is no longer to be treated by its opponents on moral and constitutional grounds, but to be contested by a despot's war; and against that war and that despot, who has murdered the peace of his country, he acknowledges all the feeling of opposition that a true and patriotic and justly indignant spirit may offer for the vindication of the right.

To vindicate the now rightful spirit of the South, and to strip despotism to its nakedness, he has written the following letters, which he hopes to continue for good. If there are harsh expressions to be found in them, it is sufficient to say that he has regretted the necessity of speaking harsh words of harsh things; and that he will be satisfied to repent the use of censure and sarcasm as untruthful, unchristian and unmanly, only when they are proved to have been undeserved.

NEAR WASHINGTON CITY, *July*, 1861.

SECOND EDITION.

A portion of the first edition of this volume, published in Maryland without the name of the author or printer, was sold in that State and in the District of Columbia—as many as one hundred having been sold in one day, by a single dealer, in the city of Baltimore. The largest portion of the edition was, however, suppressed and destroyed by the author himself, under personal constraints of necessity.

In offering a renewed edition of these letters to the people of the Confederate States, the author claims for them, aside from any personal interest, with respect to the parties to whom they are addressed, some value as related to the historical literature of the war, particularly in exposing the circumstances of its inauguration, and the policy which has conducted it from its beginning to the full and precise declaration of its objects. The volume of letters, from the fall of Sumter to the date of the meeting of the last Congress at Washington, completes, in fact, what is the most important, because the initiatory part, of the history of the war.

RICHMOND, VA., *November*, 1861.

INDEX.

		PAGE.
I.	Letter to President Lincoln, written at Washington,	9
II.	Letter to President Lincoln, written at Washington,	17
III.	Letter to President Lincoln, written at Washington,	26
IV.	Letter to President Lincoln, written near the Government,	33
V.	Letter to the Editor of ...., written in Maryland,	44
VI.	Letter to Secretary Seward, written in Maryland,	52
VII.	Letter to President Lincoln, written in Maryland,	63
VIII.	Letter to Doctor Tyng, written in Baltimore,	75
IX.	Letter to General Scott, written in Maryland,	85
X.	Letter to Mr. Everett, written in Maryland,	89

LETTERS OF THE SOUTHERN SPY.

I.

LETTER TO THE PRESIDENT.

WASHINGTON CITY, D. C., APRIL 13, 1861.

To the President of the United States:

SIR: Permit me to address you respectfully, but none the less earnestly; for neither the magnitude of the events which happened this day, nor the thoughts of a freeman's patriotism at any time, can be satisfied with expressions concealed or softened, except to that point of respect due to magisterial office.

I can testify to you, sir, my poignant regrets, as a lover of my country, and even as a Christian lover of peace, at the collision at Sumter. But these feelings are not without a reference of my judgment to where the responsibility for the actual commencement of hostilities may lie; though it may be that recriminations cannot lessen the force of patriotic regrets, or control the consequences of what is already accomplished. I am aware, sir, that the belligerent supporters of your Administration counterfeit a sense of satisfaction in the plea of the government acting on "the defensive"—a plea which you yourself have again affirmed to-day in your reply to the Virginia commissioners. Unfortunately for you, sir, the plea is weakened by the force of the circumstance that the Government, in the first instance, might have avoided a conflict, and that the real responsibility reaches back to the threshold of the controversy. The policy of war has been determined, necessarily determined, not by the bombardment of Fort Sumter, but by earlier events, that plainly and voluntarily led to this result and furnished its provocation.

I should suppose, sir, that when a party does what he knows to be a *sure* act of provocation, it is quite equivalent to the first blow, on the principle, which is familiar to small lawyers, if not to statesmen, that a man intends the natural (and still more strongly, if anticipated) consequences of his acts.

The country will explore the source, and therefore the real seat of the responsibility. It will look back to the primary cause of war, without resting on those secondary events which have no responsible character in themselves, because determined, procured, and looked for in the very outset of the policy of which they are the fruits.

It cannot be doubted, sir, that you procured the battle of Sumter; you had no desire or hope to retain the fort; you neglected to fight, until every chance of doing so with success had passed away; and when at last you did draw your sword against the sovereignty of South Carolina, the circumstances of the battle, the non-participation of your fleet in it, show that it was not a contest for victory, but only a shallow trick to entitle you to the advantages to be derived from an action for assault and battery. It was, sir, a trick—a trick to transfer easily, and under false pretences, the matters in dispute between the two sections from the arbitrament of reason to that of arms. How is it that you hope to make yourself not responsible for this unnatural and shocking appeal to war? Was not your formal intimation to the Montgomery Government that you were about to resort to force, a challenge to arms? Could the

South have been expected to disregard such a challenge? Or, if, sir, you were only amusing yourself with idle menace, are you any the less culpable because you excited a quarrel by bullying instead of bravery? Your responsibility for the commencement of hostilities, sir, is already a historical fact, and completes the character of your policy as one of blunders, perfidy and blood-guiltiness.

Had you, sir, acknowledged the independence of the seceded States—*acknowledged it for purposes of pacification*—you might have accomplished what war cannot only never obtain for you, but of what it will surely rob you. You might have kept the support of the intelligent and commanding portion of your party. You would certainly have secured the sympathies of the border States. You would have erected a standard under which the masses of Union men in the South, who never could be expected to rally under a standard of war, could have served to a man. You would have reduced the excitement that threatened the Government to channels leading to the happy and naturally aided restoration of peace.

Now, "all is lost, *save honor*"—not honor as the knightly King who wrote the phrase intended it, but "the honor" of having "acted under the forms of the Constitution" in a fratricidal war! The government that, in the broad and liberal enlightenment of modern times, seeks to administer constitutional and public law on a policy of punctilios, is none the less behind the age, whether in Central Europe or on the shores of the Atlantic. The advisers of such courses of statesmanship have not read the lessons of history aright—not even the latest. You yourself, sir, must have forgotten the lessons even of the Italian war. You forgot that the kingdom of Italy has been ushered so lately into existence through the very teeth of the treaties of Vienna. You forget that Austria has reaped the fruits of the policy recommended to you, and found them, to her cost, in insisting on the punctilios of those treaties—the most boasted part of the "public law of Europe"—to maintain a "war footing" in her Italian possessions, and in losing them by the very effort to make her authority more secure.

Look to our own war of independence. Those who have despised and declaimed against the policy of an acknowledgment, or even a *quasi* acknowledgment (no matter what the guise or the purpose) on the part of your Government of the independence of the seceded States, forget the history and traditions of those times. The policy referred to does not present the specious question, as they would have you, at least, if not the country, believe, of governmental honor or dishonour—certainly no more than the acknowledgment of the independence of the American colonies, advocated by a portion of the Whig party, presented the alternative of honor or dishonor to the British Crown. Do you suppose, sir, that Pitt and his noble coadjutors were any the less Englishmen, or patriots, or statesmen, for having attempted to resist the unnatural and unprofitable war which the British government was preparing to make upon the seceded colonies? Or can it be said in this day (although it possibly might have been said formerly by tory papers) that when Lord Effingham and the eldest son of the Earl of Chatham threw up their commissions in the army rather than serve in a war against their colonial brethren; and when General Oglethrope refused the splendid bribe of the office of commander-in-chief of the British forces against America, that they acted in a traitorous or ignoble spirt, or bore the taint of cowardice upon their names. For myself, I believe that these examples of generosity, of far-seeing patriotism, patient under insults and clamor and misrepresentation, may give the most proper lessons to the captious and belligerent "patriotism" of our own day. Had Great Britain rightly observed them, she would have saved herself the blood and treasure of a seven years' war. Would that she had listened to the appeals of the colonies, when they declared, through the Continental Congress of 1775, that "they had not raised armies with the ambitious design of separating from Great Britain; and that they should lay their arms down when hostilities should cease on the part of the aggressors, and all danger of their renewal should be removed!" She did not listen, and she drove them into independence. Be assured, sir, that your Government has yet to have the lesson enforced upon it, that the spirit of independence, misconceived or not, is but developed by war, with the unavoidable circumstance of insisting, at each stage of its progress, on new and further demands, when the first movements might have well been held in check by the simple energy of patience.

    Respectfully,
       THE SOUTHERN SPY.

II.

LETTER TO THE PRESIDENT.

Washington City, D. C., April 16, 1861.

To the President of the United States:

Sir: Your proclamation of war is before the country; and the spirit that dictated it is already caught up in the revengeful exultations of Black Republican presses over the prospect of blood. I say *blood*, sir; for however you may gainsay it, or jest about it, it is the curse of fratricidal blood that you have pronounced, distinctly and irrevocably. I say *jest*, sir; for surely you did but jest, when you said in your inaugural that you would take the forts and arsenals (like Shylock's pound of flesh) without a drop of bloodshed; and you did but jest, when, with the cannon peals of Sumter on the air, you protested to the Virginia commissioners that you would modify your inaugural, only so far as to "perhaps cause the United States mails to be withdrawn" from the seceded States; and you do now but jest when mustering to fields of civil war a *land* force of seventy-five thousand men, you yet proclaim that the places of the government only are to be repossessed, and that "the utmost care" is to be taken to "avoid any devastation, any destruction of or interference with, property, or any disturbance of peaceful citizens in any part of the country!" Alas, sir, have you nothing better to offer to an agonized country than the same flimsy and harlequin disguises of the trifler, with which you tricked yourself out for the entertainment of the crowds of idlers that watched your progress to the capital? Nothing very terrible to happen— no devastation—no disturbances, and yet an army of seventy-five thousand men called to your command for service on land, and the most monstrous proportions of civil war already erected in staring ghastliness over the whole country! Sir, this is not ingenuous—it is not appropriate—it is, I tell you, sir, the trifling of the jester in the Chamber of Death!

So far as the legal aspects of your proclamation are concerned, you have violated the laws in the very appeal you make to them. You have usurped the power of Congress to declare war.

You have called out the militia, not as the act of 1795 (which the law adviser of your government has vainly sought to distort for your purposes) indicates, in aid of the civil authorities, but to supersede them, and to inaugurate war in its most deformed nakedness. You have attempted, too, to make the militia of this district subject not only to the rules and articles of war in point of *discipline*, which is the legal limit of your authority, but to denude them of the character of citizen soldiery, to swear them by oaths to your person, and to constitute them into prætorian bands. This may be military genius, and decision; but to a plain man it seems like military despotism. A war begun and invoked in the name of law, and yet disregarding the law even in the ceremonies of its inauguration, promises nothing but shame and disaster.

But suppose, sir, that the most unbounded success should attend your arms; suppose you should heap up the most immense treasures of victory and blood, where, after all, would be your gains? You cannot reclaim sovereign States, except as conquests; and as conquests, they would be to you worse than useless.

Why, then, sir—and the question is very simple—make that an occasion of war, where war would be unnatural, and in the end, wholly unprofitable? Even when a government is an empire, instead of a confederation, there may be occasions where the acknowledgment of the independence of a seceded province, even, resolved on independence, may be policy, and statesmanship, and patriotism. Is it any the less so now than when Great Britain was besought by her best patriots to restrain herself from war upon her American colonies, and to concede their demands. You, sir, and your party, profess to believe the South a spotted and degraded section, doing dishonor to the name and position before the world of what was once our common country. Why, then, seek to reclaim these people to your intercourse? Why pursue them in their retreat? Pharoah attempted to reclaim the hated Israelites, that they might not go out of the land of Egypt. But, mark you, he sought to reclaim them as *slaves!*

Is, sir, your own heart surely hardened like that of the Egyptian king? Let me remind you, sir, if not, perhaps, a student of your Bible, of the outlines of that awful drama by the Red sea. It was there, on the boundary of battle, that Moses spoke to his countrymen, who cried in their fear to return to the land of bondage, and, in the clear heroic terms of his own towering faith and courage, gave the command: "Fear ye not, stand still; for the Egyptians whom ye have seen to day, ye shall shall see them no more forever!"

You have appealed to the issues of war! Let those issues, then, decide! When the reason and the better feelings of a man, or even a "President," are stifled, it will be useless to preach to him even the lessons of the Bible.

The fact, sir—the fact which, at once, reveals the infamous desire of the war you have inaugurated, and the immensity of the prize in issue for the South—is that that unhappy section has been used to contribute the bulk of the revenues of the government, to build up the North, and to enrich her enemies by every form of tribute. The Northern plutocratic power would have it continued so. It would still derive its forty to fifty millions of annual revenue from the South, through the operations of the tariff; it would, still, batten on the Southern trade in its markets, a recent aggregate of which is stated at four hundred millions of dollars a year; it would still, from unequal taxations, and different sources of tribute in the intercourse between the sections, reap its immense harvest of gain, which a Northern writer has calculated at over two hundred millions of dollars per year, and which, sir, represents the annual aggregate tax or cost of the "glorious Union" to the South.

It is this prize, wrapped in the pretences of Stars and Stripes, for which you will contend; and believe me, sir, it is, for this also that the South will press its war, and out of which it can afford to pay the extremest expenses of that war.

You, sir, now, after the elaborate illustration of your traits of statesmanship, will have the advantage of showing other resources of your extraordinary character, and of exhibiting, what you are said to possess, the splendid stores of your military genius. You have commenced well, sir. You are a stern master—a most excellent military ruler. You are already a Nero in your own capital.

I congratulate you upon your almost perfect establishment of military terrorism over a parasitical city. You have filled your capital with troops. You have set up a political inquisition in Washington, by the process of military TEST OATHS, wringing from men's consciences all that is precious to men's freedom. You have opened markets on the green in front of the War Department to buy of starving men in your capital, for soldier's pay and rations, their bodies, and principles, and consciences. You have surrounded yourself with every element to inspire terror around you. Your minions and your parasites are this day hunting through the streets of Washington, to do violence, by threats, at least, to every man who dares to oppose your Administration. And, for the first time, and, as I firmly believe, for the last time, in the history of our country, a Government, still holding on to the old name and the old traditions of our national independence, is striving to cow under the very shadow of the capital—the ancient mansion of American liberty—the ancient freedom of sentiment and of utterance.

But, sir, beware! The terrorism is not yet complete in your capital. It is true that many of those, who, when danger was distant, were loudest and bravest in the censure of you and your party, are satisfied now to sneak around the streets of Washington, anxious to play the part of "*hen hussies*" for the women and children, speaking with "bated breath," or pleading new scruples for submission, with the slime of their cowardice tracking them through the crowd. But let me assure you, sir, that there are in the midst of your federal city men of a different character and purpose—men who know their rights—and men who rejoice with more than Roman pride, that whether they stand on a foreign soil, or beneath the folds of their seven-starred banner, they stand as free citizens, under the protection of their own free republic. You will not subdue them. You cannot coerce them. You will be sorry to touch a hair of their heads.

Take care, too, that the terrorism you have established in Washington does not react upon yourself. Do not tremble for your person, sir! I do not mean *that*. But I do warn you that the reign of terror, already inaugurated in Washington, stands, this day, as a despotic example before the country; that revolt may soon stand you, face to face, in your capital; and that the time may come when Washington, oppressed and crushed down by tyranny, and beleaguered by armies, fresh from fields of victory, will have nothing to oppose to them but the wretched bodies and vagabond uniforms of starving janizaries. Then, sir, tremble—*tremble!*

The splendid and chivalrous Roman Tribune, that founded the latter Rome, consented to escape from the throne of the Cæsars in the disguise of a baker; but it was only when the walls of his Capitol were falling around him, and the sounds of its ruins was already in his ears. Will you, sir, wait until then?—or will you, with nerves already shattered by your midnight escapade to the shallow refuges of Washington, choose to escape now?

I am, &c.,

THE SOUTHERN SPY.

III.

LETTER TO THE PRESIDENT.

Washington City, D. C., April 20, 1861.

To the President of the United States:

Sir: In one sense, I must congratulate you: in another, permit me to express my pity for you.

The masked author of "Junius" tells us that the counsels and expedients of *party*, rather than higher principles of policy, determined for England the war upon her colonies; and that the procurers of this war, while intending only the ruin of an opposition in parliament, " in effect divided one-half of the empire from the other."

A victory, sir, culminating in such grand historical results, you, yourself, have just illustrated. The time has come when it is clearly seen that you have done your strictest duty to your party. A simple man, possessed only of that degree of intelligence that may be expected to be acquired in the contracted and vulgar life of a Western village, you have conceived no vain ideas of statesmanship above the integrity of "the Chicago platform," and have disdained all counsellors beyond your associations with "the thorough" Republicans of your party. In the spirit of fidelity to party, you have determined the issue of war for your country. You know very well that the Union is peace; that you cannot establish it by arms. You know very well that glory is to be wrested only from a foreign enemy; and that it is never to be purchased from the victories of a civil war. You have made war, sir, neither for the reparations of evils, nor for the glory of arms. You have made it at the command of a political party resolved "to rule or to ruin."

Enjoy, sir, the felicities of your situation. You have obeyed the behests of your party: hasten to prepare yourself for their servile congratulations. The men who have hurried you to the exploit of war, will not spare their praises. The vile priest of the Abaddon, who prays his god for "war redder than blood," will set you up as an idol among the demon glories of his religion. The mobs will cry "Hosannah." Even the ken-marked and hobbling wretch, who edits the great organ of Abolition for your party in the North, will exhaust himself to spew over you his clotted praises, as if in some sort of beastly adoration of your person!

But, sir, let this be the limit of your rejoicing. The Union is lost forever. The jewelled States of the South are lost to you, and gained for Independence forever. A war confronts you to proclaim that independence in your ears, and to drive you, with denuded crown, from the soil that it is about to consecrate to the eternal liberties of the South.

"His majesty," said the great commoner, prophesying the liberty of the American Colonies on the floor of parliament—"his majesty may wear his crown, but, without the American jewel in it, it will not be worth wearing."

It is said that you are even already alarmed for the safety of your person, on account of circumstances daily surrounding you to make you a prisoner, in spite of Northern succors, in your own capital. I pity you, sir. I might have told you, months ago, that the South had no fear of any war you might make, and that the effort of your proclamation to frighten her people, and even your twenty days' grace to "the combinations" would not strike the sudden terror or submission in their hearts that you anticipated. You may satisfy yourself with a short-lived tyranny, with desultory atrocities, with a display of arms; but, plainly, sir, you are not the man to sustain a war in the nineteenth century, in the interest of an usurped government, and in opposition to a people, resolved to take their own destinies into their own hands.

I am glad for the sake of my country, sir, to be satisfied on reflection that the war you will wage will be contracted in its powers beyond what you anticipated. It is said that you have abundant offers of Northern succor; that twenty thousand men in the coalpits of Pennsylvania, alone, have offered you their services; and that you even boast of your opportunity to introduce a religious element to exasperate the war, by hiring German Protestants, "to a man," and animating them against the true and steadfast Catholic patriots of the country. But, sir, all these are but the boasts of a weak cause—the rhodomontade of the streets of Washington. Be pacified, sir. Your Dutch troops will find employment enough in guarding the passes of the Long Bridge, and in poking bayonets at half-breeched newsboys about the Departments, without entering upon the task of a massacre of the Irish.

Look, sir, to the South. Are we to believe that your proclamation, received in Montgomery with derisive laughter, scorned by North Carolina and Kentucky, with all the speed with which the lightning of the telegraph could bring their messages of defiance to you, thrown back in your face by Virginia, with the treatening stamp of her foot already on the banks of the Potomac—can even you, sir, believe that this mighty proclamation has subdued one throb of Southern courage, or subtracted one man from the lists of her cause of independence! No, sir, it has multiplied them. Your effort to alarm the South has only alarmed yourself. Your collection of Northern troops, numerous it may be, but unanimated to fight by any of those sentiments, which give victory in battle, has but given new accessions and new ardors to a people fighting for their liberties, and possessing all that confidence, and all those great moral principles of victory inspired by a war of independence.

I thank God, sir, that my own native State,

Virginia, is, this day, not listening to the timeserver. What her Convention may determine I know not; but I know that her lineal people will, ultimately determine nothing to the dishonor of their glorious State—nothing in the shallow spirit of cowardice, or of mean compliance with present power. Virginia will not listen to counsels conceived in such a spirit. She will listen, let me assure you, sir, to higher sources of inspiration than your own—to the voices of her history—to the commands of her mission—to the thunder-toned messages that, commenced at Sumter, will soon peal around the peninsula of the Atlantic. Break the unity of the South! She never will. Fold her arms with wailing cries of "peace!" She never will. Take argued repose from you! She never will. Stand still when the battle is on the air, and the ground is sown with the blood of her brethren! She never—never will.

Sir, you cannot terrify the South. In vain will her people explore your own character, for evidences of the conqueror. You may be a sanguinary man. You exhibit no traits of being a warlike one. Guarded by prætorian bands in your capital; encompassed with ten armed attendants, it is said, in your sleeping room; with liberty to practice still all the levities of your character, even in the darkest hours of your country's agony and suffering; not even intermitting your drawing-room entertainment on the evening of the day of the commencement of the civil war at Sumter, you do, indeed, resemble Nero, the blood-thirsty trifler, not Cæsar, the conqueror.

Sir, I am sorry to disappoint your vanity, or to abate your courage. But the truth, the fact—the exclamation of pity for you, and the prophecy of victory in the war of liberty—is, that *the South does not fear you!*

I am, &c.,

THE SOUTHERN SPY.

IV.

LETTER TO THE PRESIDENT.

NEAR THE GOVERNMENT, APRIL 27, 1861.

The President of the United States:

SIR: You are said to flatter yourself that you have now succeeded in expelling from Washington all who have dared to utter a word in opposition to your Administration. It is true that you have driven many of them out by armed mobs invested with the gilded livery of your service. Stationed on the highways and the by-ways, they have sought to kidnap men or to buy their souls for your service; divided into innumerable press-gangs they have daily explored the groggeries for victims; detailed as spies, they have constantly furnished to you, or your minions, lists for proscription; or straggling about the streets as liveried bullies, they have sought to entrap men into private quarrels, or to force them to self-defence, that the mob in waiting might overpower and murder them. Such, sir, is the condition of subjection to your imperial will to which you flatter yourself that you have reduced the city of Washington. The country will remember its history. It will remember that it has been accomplished while your partisans, including even the ruffian knight of Kansas, who guards with a hundred men your convivial night hours, have been holding meetings in the sacred precincts of the churches of Washington, to insist upon and to exclaim upon, with the old puritanical ribaldry of righteousness, *free speech* for "the Lord's people," but for none besides.

But, sir, you flatter yourself with one mistake. Many of the enemies whom you think to have expelled by your military mobs, have left Washington on other accounts. They hope to see you again. The mission of the National Volunteers was fulfilled in your capital before they left it, or before the minor organ of your Administration essayed to procure their arrest. Be careful, moreover, sir, how you give yourself up so entirely to the belief that all your enemies in Washington are expelled or subdued to fear—"*Your lists are not yet full enough,*" cried the weary and trembling Robespierre to his secretaries, after months had been vainly spent in assuring, by the extent of his proscriptions, the Reign of Terror in the capital of France. They *were* not full enough. A few days passed, and the gaunt and cowardly tyrant of Paris was in the hands of the avengers, and borne along the streets with the shout of the "*guillotine*" in his ears.

However entertaining it may be to some minds to observe the terrors of a tyrant, or to witness their realization, permit me, sir, to pass to notice some other lessons which you have given to the country in the condition of things you have maintained at your capital. In the small district where your authority is, for the moment, supreme, you have naturally given the truest examples of your theory and designs of government for the whole country. They are examples in which the wantonness of a Republican majority, the terrors of the cowardice of its leaders, exhibitions of military terrorism, oaths of feudal allegiance, and the subordinations of patriotism to the servile sentiments of vassalage contend for preëminence in the display. They are, in short, the most proper examples of the despotism which you desire to establish over the whole country, and in which you essay to maintain its union.

When will the country learn that your idea of maintaining the old Union of the States is simply despotic—conceived in no historical enthusiasm for restoring past glories—animated by no patriotic desires contemplating the good of the whole country—but coldly and sternly calculated in the narrow spirit of the despot. I do not accuse you, sir, without a record. Your own speeches—and those speeches intended, too, as special explanations of your purposes—condemn you. When you were visited by a committee of the clergy of Baltimore, with messages and implorations for peace, you answered them in a style too vulgar and trifling to show the least real regard either for the Union or the peace of the country. In the accounts of such a conference, it was to be hoped that at least one historical sentiment might have dropped from your lips, or some words of grave, or, at least, decent concern for the destinies of the country. But the country was disappointed even in the small expectation of decency in your manners. You are said to have expressed no concern, but that for the safety of your person; to have given no other explanation of the war you were waging than a desire to secure the revenues of the South still to the coffers of your treasury; and to have had the effrontery, at last, to declare in the same breath in which you proclaimed your fears and cowardice, that you were determined to maintain your reputation for "*spunk*" in the prosecution of hostilities. Alas, sir, consider the spectacle: A committee before you, dignified by the holy offices of religion, and yet more dignified by their special mission of charity, entreating, in the last emergency, the restraint of the war you had declared, and you answering them with the explanations of that war in the needs of the treasury and your panic fears of being hanged, and with the wretched phrases and anecdotes of vulgar wit! I will not dwell on such a spectacle.

The accounts, sir, of your interview with the Baltimore committee are only paralleled, as they may be, in a measure, explained by the well known habits of your life in the retreats of the executive mansion. It is, indeed, a curious fact of history, that the worst tyrants have been remarkable for their levities of behavior, and have rather increased in the most terrible distresses of their country the frivolities and enjoyments of their palaces. You, sir, are sa'd to illustrate this imperial peculiarity in the occupations of jest and conviviality in the White House, at the very time you are contemplating the proscriptions and massacres of your countrymen. You are no more willing to give up the trifles and privileged buffooneries of your position than to yield the substantial symbols of your power. You are not willing to return to your old resources in the taverns of Springfield. You wish to remain the trifler and tyrant of the White House; consoled by "experienced nurses" (whom Miss Dix has promised you); compelling "the old soldier," who protects you, to low familiarities with your person; and comforting yourself with the vulgar gloatings of the bully over the terrors of those who are afraid only because they are more cowardly than himself.

Indeed, such are the trivialities of your disposition, sir, that I can testify that you have not even yet restrained the pleasant liberty of the lady of the White House to prosecute her purchases in the "dollar stores" on the avenue. Twice this week I have had the pleasure of observing her there in the feminine elation of cheap "bargains."

But to return, sir, to a very brief analysis of your disclosures to your Baltimore visitors. We are left to understand by them that your motives for war are double: to save your revenue in the South, and to assure the protection of your person. If, in the compass of possibilities, you should attain the first—conquer the South to that point whereat you might be able to collect, by force, a revenue in her borders—consider that it could only be at the price of massacres which could never be repaid, and with the loss of all the great interests which may be enumerated in the peace and liberty of a country. If you should accomplish the second motive—the individual safety of Abraham Lincoln—it would be, sir, still more questionable in what respect your country would be a gainer.

If the regards fo your personal safety are really uppermost in your mind, why not, sir, effect them by the obvious means already at your command? Why not declare for peace? It might instantly restore the safety of your person. Why not resign, making your resignation on such conditions, or with such understandings with your constitutional successors as to call for a new election to the chief executive office? It, under present circumstances, would be the master-stroke of your life. It would be but giving to the people, impressively and directly, a question too grave for any one man to decide. It would leave you without the reproaches of weakness, and with the undying honors of having submitted a civil war to the last resort of arbitrament. It would imitate the conservative and virtuous feature of the British Government (which, in many respects, was the model for our own,) in the capacity it has, by a change of ministry, which is virtually the governing power, to adapt itself to changes of circumstances, and to conform itself, at all times, to public sentiment. It would—if this consideration can plead to you above all—save your person with decency and with certainty. But no, sir—you will not adopt these obvious and honorable modes of escape. The truth is, you are anxious to save your person, but you are anxious to save it as that of an enthroned despot.

Do I not, sir, rightly interpret your feelings, or do I err in verbal accuracy in calling such a war of "safety" a war of *despotism*. Look back, sir, only to the date of your proclamation, and you will see that you have already fulfilled all the conditions of a war of bad faith and aggression, and already confirmed, beyond the possibility of a doubt, the character of your hostilities as those of a tyrant.

When you made your proclamation, you then indicated that the forces you summoned therein, were to be used to repossess the forts on the Southern coasts. You have already falsified this declaration of purpose. Under new pretences of protecting Washington, you have completely turned attention from the Southern forts, to invest Virginia and Maryland with your forces. Washington is but the strategical point of the campaign. It will enable you to seize Alexandria, to command the important heights of the Potomac, and to occupy the Northern portions of Virginia with subsidiary forces. On the other hand, the possession of the equally important point of Fortress Monroe is calculated to give you command of the low countries of Virginia.

You are already in possession of the two important passages into Virginia. You have secured a safe and uninterrupted transit through Maryland, not willing, as yet, to risk the Thermopylæ of Baltimore. You have not only violated the sovereignty of Maryland in the usurpation of an absolute right of way, but that right, which you insisted upon for yourself, you have been prompt to deny to the people of the State itself! Your forces are to have free transit through the territories of Maryland, but the people of Maryland are not to enjoy the same right in their own territories. They are already cut off from Washington, and from Annapolis, while your own troops pass uninterruptedly between these points.

These movements, sir, betray the designs of an aggressive war waged by a desperate tyrant. You are said to boast already that, with the command of the Chesapeake, and of the larger portion of the Potomac boundary, to have effectually cut off the connection between Maryland and Virginia, and with Washington and Fortress Monroe in your possession, to "*hold the wolf by the ears.*" We shall soon test the justice of your boast:

we already know and appreciate the spirit of despotic subjugation in which it is uttered.

Virginia, sir, may have been betrayed into some degree of inertness by the false implications of your proclamation; and there may have been traitors in her own borders to help her to the false conclusion of maintaining what is called a "*defensive*" position. But the brave and enthusiastic spirit of her people will soon override the formularies of delay and of that caution in which treachery often finds at once its own concealment, and the means of seducing others. It will, it must soon confront you on the banks of the Potomac; it will, it must, at the last, brave you in your capital; it will, it must, as sure as the prophecies of necessity, lay your proud city in such ruins, as will leave nothing hereafter to be fought for. *Carthago delenda est.* Remember the end; it approaches; it involves your own destiny—perhaps the life you have nursed with guards and bolts, and fattened with convivial joys, only for a sacrifice for the sword of the avenger.

I am, &c.,

THE SOUTHERN SPY.

V.

LETTER TO THE EDITOR OF ....

MARYLAND, MAY 1, 1861.

To the Editor of ....

SIR: It is related of an ancient wagoner that having got his vehicle into a difficult pass, he implored Jupiter to extricate him. After long importunities in prayer to the god, to show him out of his difficulties, he, at last, received the simple answer, "*put your shoulder to the wheel.*"

The bemired State of Maryland is imploring to be delivered from the difficulties, and terrors of her position. Let me say, the only way to do it, is to "put the shoulder to the wheel;" and while men delay to do this, it is plain she will only sink deeper in the mire and mold of her position.

It is strange indeed, that men of Maryland, who were going about a few days ago with the *decantatum* of "secession" on their lips, are now struck with a sudden stupor. They say that they can do nothing, that they are powerless, that the reversion of public sentiment, under the influence of the fears of the people, is now irresistible.

The fact is, sir, that there is a reversion, and a reversion which is one of the most naked and shameless tergiversations of the times. While too many are satisfied to rest the cause of liberty on mere protestations of feeling, or on idle invocations for help, a constant appeal is being made by others to the fears of the State, to drive her back into the refuges of the Union: all manly sentiment, all generous sympathies, and that spirit of devotion which is the spirit of independence, are choked by spectral fears, or crushed in the selfish and narrow considerations of the present.

Maryland is advised to try no "crucial experiments," but to betake herself to the safe position of a temporising policy, in which she may give the advantages of her neutral position to the Lincoln Government, and yield the privileges of her soil for the present, to its troops, and, possibly, hereafter join the Southern Confederacy, but only in the event of the successful establishment, or the acknowledgment of its independence. This dishonorable, cheating, double position—this precious, safe game of ambidextrous neutrality—is now the constant theme of recommendation that assails the ear. Even one of the hitherto most excellent and patriotic journals of Baltimore is now prompt to recommend the duplicity and advantages of such a position. The copy of this journal which lies before me at the date of this writing, advises a pledge of good faith, made on the honor of the State and without reservation, not to take up arms against the Federal Administration, so long as the city of Washington is held and occupied by them; nor to offer any hostility or opposition to the Administration, or the army assembled for its support upon the soil of Maryland. It adds in cold, confident, shameless terms the following explanation of its choice:

"The result of this position would secure to "the Administration the enjoyment of all the ad-"vantages to be derived from the territory of a "neutral, with the assurance of absolute safety "within that territory; and with the possible "maintenance of peaceful relations until the "Union was restored, if that be practicable, or "*until the independence of the Southern Confed-*"*cracy is recognized.*"

Such wretched ambiloquy as this—such a miserable cheat as this is sought to be imposed upon the honor of Maryland, and the honor of that cause, which she proposes to pollute by mercenary and chaffering embraces. God forbid that this should be the choice of Maryland! God forbid that she should sell her destinies and honor to any of the infamous bids to pollute her—to the cheats of the press; or to the suggestions of terrorism; or to Gov. Hicks' plain-spoken proposition to debauch her; or to the gold of "the commercial centres" of the North, already busy in corrupting her honest choice; or to the cunning toils of the wizen-faced King of Plug-Uglyism, who seeks to purchase by Maryland's infamy the seat in Congress that he has already assoiled by his own treachery!

Sir, I cannot write with patience of these attempts to betray a State, whose heart and honor are alike noble. Excuse me for my warmth. And pray understand, also, my own position on this question, not as that of recommending instant and reckless secession to Maryland, but of advising only active, willing, laborious, thorough, and spirited preparations for what in the end must be, and should be her position. Her sister

States of the South appreciate the present, helpless situation of Maryland, and do not ask, as they cannot expect, her immediate separation from the Union; but they do expect that she will not be idle, or submissive, or indifferent, but that she will prepare herself; that she will arm herself; and that in undiminished spirit she will await the time, when she may declare herself, purely and bravely, and, above all, without mean reference to what side victory inclines to, a member of the Southern Confederacy of States.

God forbid that any should be so unjust, or so athirst of blood as to condemn the present enforced suspension of her action. But I condemn, sir, the designs of her enemies to take advantage of the present necessary spell to place her in a position of irretrievable and certain submission to the misgovernment of the North. I condemn the cheat of imposing upon her the farce of a one-sided neutrality, unable to protect itself, and the next necessary step of which will be union with the North. And I alike condemn that pretence of neutrality, which is to enable her to adopt, in the course of events, whichever side is proved to be the stronger, and which, while professing desire for the connection of Maryland with the Southern States, makes itself safe by reserving the alternative of siding with the Lincoln Government, in the event of their discouragement.

It is unnecessary to expose here the positions of Gov. Hicks' message. Sir, it is not worth the prick of a pen to disturb it. Whatever the Legislature of Maryland may do, it is some satisfaction to know that it will be entirely without reference to his recommendations; and whatever scheme may be determined by it to advise or provide for the *suspension* of the State's action, it will, at least, be unlike the clotted lump of nonsense, which he has recommended as "neutrality."

Very truly, yours,

THE SOUTHERN SPY.

Maryland, May 16, 1861. * * * * * * * *
Since the above letter was written, Maryland has fallen further within the grasp of the despot. About thirty thousand foreign troops are on her soil to-day; the Legislature has been wholly inane, and has assented to the attitude of submission *indefinitely;* the city of Baltimore has been subjected to military occupation and to the insults,

for a time at least, of the dawdling and inebriate proclamations of an obese, epauletted Yankee; and while efforts have been plainly in progress to disarm the State, and to violate her military organization, her shuffling Governor has sought safe occasion to ape the tyranny he obeys, and to make a call for four regiments of volunteers to answer the requisition of the now old and spent war proclamation, made a month ago by the cousin of humanity perched in the Executive Chair at Washington. The soldiers, the apes, the time-servers, and the mummies, are the curse of Maryland. And what of the patriotic, liberty-loving men of the unhappy State!—Said a hero in the trials of the Revolution of 76: "too many flatter themselves that their pusillanimity is true prudence; but in perilous times like these, I cannot conceive of prudence without fortitude!"—that is not active bravery and prowess, which are sometimes untimely, but *"fortitude:"* the patient, confident, heroic spirit, which, while it waits for opportunity, makes both it and the preparations to use it. Let Maryland act on this hint—let her make, as best she can, both the opportunity and the preparation to strike home with the avenging arm—let her preserve and exercise her fortitude—let her do this; or let her assume at once a repose of irretrievable infamy! *Nullum est tertium.*

S. S.

VI.

LETTER TO SECRETARY SEWARD.

MARYLAND, MAY 10, 1861.

To Mr. Secretary Seward:

SIR: You have been for many years an object of public curiosity. Excelling in the concealments and disguises of empty declamation, remarkable for the glosses of your style of expression, and exhibiting that command of language which makes it perform the office of concealing rather than expressing thoughts, and which was so happily illustrated in your well-known composition of the Inaugural of the Illinois President, your sentiments and your character have been very differently estimated in the opinion of the public. You have been regarded as a statesman it the parts of the North, where people, judging from their own stand-points of character, have esteemed statesmanship to consist in low cunning and artful non-committals of evil designs; and to them your very New England visage of narrow and skulking selfishness has been taken as an index of Yankee wisdom and ability. By others, sir, who profess to have pierced the disguises of your character, you are condemned as a *demagogue*, a character baneful in the days of peace, but in the great peril of a country, then the most heartless mercenary and dangerous of wretches.

I am truly sorry, sir, to see this latter estimation of your character confirmed by your recent exhibitions of the narrow and demagogical statesmanship that you have so long sought to conceal. An acute man may long find resources of concealment in ambiguous and artful words; but the word and spirit of his expressions, especially should he be over-fond of talking and writing, will eventually betray his sentiments and designs to the mind of the people.

In the last Senate, you made a glowing appeal for the Union; you confessed it to be in danger; you besought sacrifices, even of party, to sustain it. You must have been only amusing the people with these declarations; for in your late official letter of instructions to the recently appointed minister to France, you urge him to assure that government of the fact that the idea of a permanent disruption has never entered into the mind of "any candid *statesman* in this country," and of the certainty, too, of the continuance of "the *constitutional* Union," and that, too, as an object of "*affection!*"

How, sir, do you explain this inconsistency? Is the Union in less danger now, when war is proclaimed, than when, in the season of conventions, you delivered your glossed and jesuitical speech in the Senate for its preservation? Is it *the fact* that no statesman in this country conceives the possibility of its rupture? Pardon me, sir, are you truthful in this? I acknowledge, sir, that there is a magnanimous part in these declations, and I congratulate you for it. You are willing to confess that you were no statesman in once contemplating the danger of the Union. You are willing to make yourself out as formerly, a fool. But, sir, will the country be satisfied to take even this magnanimous confession: for, remember, sir, there is yet a more scornful name than that of fool, and for calling which, inconsistency sometimes affords equal grounds.

You have abandoned your exclamatory statesmanship for the Union to adopt in its stead the wisdom of your master, and to substitute for your former anxieties his vulgar apothegms of "*all right,*" "*nobody hurt,*" and "*nothing going wrong.*" You are, indeed, a supple tool. Now when the Union is imminently threatened, you exchange the fears you had for it, when it was only moderately threatened, for Abraham Lincoln's vulgar and insolent confidence, on which you improve by the art which is peculiarly your own. You misrepresent. You misrepresent a great government, inaugurated under the solemn and imposing forms of State authority; already sustained by nearly eight millions of people; exercising among them all the ordinary functions of government, and receiving their willing obedience, and standing before the world for rightful recognition—you misrepresent it as a disorganized insurrection, from which nothing is to be feared, and you rank it with the passing and incidental "changes" in the history of the Union.

This, sir, is in consistency, at least, with the war proclamation of Abraham Lincoln, of which I can now well believe the report that you were the scrivener. In that proclamation, which had to be bungled into conformity to a tortured law and to a perverse misrepresentation of facts, it was necessary to style States acting under the solemnities of organic bodies, as "unlawful *combinations;*" and to support, still further, the affectation of a mere raid, we had to be refreshed with another Lincolniana, in warning four or five millions of people, standing on their own soil, to return within twenty days to their *homes!* What an example of seriousness, of truthfulness, of justice, of patriotic courage and patriotic rhetoric, I leave the world to admire.

I am willing to admit, sir, that the misrepresentations you couched in this famous proclamation, and that you have attempted now to renew to the Governments of Europe, would be most richly, as they are most impotently, ridiculous, if they were not so foul with falsehood, as to excite disgust as well as derision. Why conceal the fact of the existence of a Government in the South, recognised within its own jurisdiction, and exercising all the powers for revenue, civil order, legislation, the administration of justice, peace and war? Why atttempt to degrade a great revolutionary fact by misrepresenting it as an insurrection or raid? You, sir, are best able to answer these questions. You know best your own purposes for degrading the Southern movement to the proportions of an incidental insurrection. You know best the extreme necessity for balking the European recognition of the Southern Confederacy. But, sir, you attempt a vain and shameless task, when you seek to encounter a question so serious and critical by attempted concealments and falsifications of facts op n to all the world, and which all the world is interested in examining.

The Governments of Europe, you may rest assured, will not take the facts regarding the condition of affairs in the South on the representations of inimical statements at Washington. They will ascertain and estimate them for themselves. Indeed, the very expedients employed in the conduct of hostilities on the part of your Government, as well at on the side of the South—blockades, letters of marque, &c.,—will constrain the European powers, so far from recognising your dwarfed representations of insurrection, sedition, &c., to govern their action on the basis of the actual existence of war, and to recognise the South as a belligerent. This, sir, you may see, opens the door at once to the recognition of a *de facto* Government.

You, sir, not only have committed yourself to a bad and superrogatory task in seeking to impose upon foreign governments your misstatements of facts in the South, but you have also traveled out of the way to communicate through the letter to Mr. Dayton, the mere opinions and sentiments of the Government at Washington to oppose the recognition of the Southern Confederacy. Such blunders and ignorance in diplomacy were scarcely to be expected from you. It was to be supposed that you were at least acquainted with the simple rules, to govern a matter of ordinary diplomatic routine. You have proved yourself another example that the greatly learned are sometimes not above the blunders and ignorances of common men. You are another Gundling—another great light in "the Tobacco Parliament," to settle public affairs. But it was to be supposed that you were, at least, not more ignorant and thrasonical than Gundlings generally are. It was to be supposed that you were, at least, aware that the question of the recognition of a *de facto* Government was to be determined by facts, and not by the opinions and views of that Government which it had succeeded. It was to be supposed that you had the small amount of knowledge to apprehend that the question of the recognition of the Southern Confederacy by Foreign Powers, was, for them, a question lying with the Southern people, and having nothing to do with the Federal Government, that is *ipso facto* foreign to those people.

The doctrine that must determine the recognition abroad of the Southern Confederacy, is so simple and severe, that it is, indeed, astonishing, sir, how you could have so mistaken it as to interpose the question with the views and opinions of the Lincoln Government, as to the reality of the Southern Confederacy. The question has nothing to do with these. It is one of fact, and that fact simply the determination whether the new Government sustains itself, and is recognized and obeyed *within the limits of the jurisdiction it claims.* It matters not whether it is a revolutionary Government; it matters not whether it is contested by a former regime; it is sufficient that it is recognized and obeyed by *its own people*, and performs steadily among them the regular functions of a Government.

To recommend a new Government for recognition abroad, it should assuredly fulfil these conditions—that is, be found in steady exercise of governmental functions, and be acknowledged and obeyed within the limits of its local jurisdiction. Beyond those lim.ts the inquiry ceases. It is the obedience of *its own people* that essentially makes the Government. It is not necessary, sir, to refer for these plain doctrines of recognition to the precedents of general history, or to the recent illumination of the whole subject in Europe by the Italian question. Our Declaration of Independence finds for us the just powers of Government in "*the consent of the governed.*"

But without looking back now to the distinguished examples of history as to the recognition of *de facto* Governments, you might at least, sir, refresh your mind by teachings so recent as those of the real statesman who was but one remove your predecessor in the high office which you now encumber with your pompous ignorance. I refer to the doctrines declared by Mr. Marcy on the Nicaraguan question, as establishing for our own Government the most recent and strictly defined precedent for the recognition of powers *de facto*, and doing so by putting the whole question on the simple doctrine of the reality and of the acknowledgment of the new Government by the consent of the people composing it.

Such, sir, are at once the guides and the assurances for the recognition of the Southern republic. I will not be led now into the discussion of their truth or probability. I have not written for the purpose of a general discussion of the doctrine of recognition, but only to show you, sir, how the plainest outlines of that doctrine have been violated by your false, intermeddling advices to the Governments of Europe. Be, at least, sir, truthful and decent in your zeal for Mr. Lincoln's Government. Be serious, sir: restore yourself to the society of third-rate politicians: do not disgrace them by having your falsehoods and cheats too plainly detected! Cease your busy misrepresentations to Foreign Governments—cease your boastful assurances of Abraham Lincoln's "one Government and one Nation"—cease your dissemination of the views of a Government, which no longer has any jurisdiction of a case that is given to the judgment of the world: and be satisfied for justice and decency alike to leave the question of the recognition of the new Government in the South, where it belongs by history, by precedent, and by right—to the impartial ascertainment of the state of facts existing within the limits it has appointed for its own jurisdiction.

I am, sir, &c.,

THE SOUTHERN SPY.

VII.

LETTER TO THE PRESIDENT.

MARYLAND, MAY 30, 1861.

To the President of the United States:

SIR: The course of despotism is that of rapid and aggravated progression. Commencing with doubtful claims of power, it hurries to plain usurpations of it, and, at last, seizes the sceptre of absolute authority. In little more than a month, your course, sir, has illustrated the rapid steps of despotism from its first unlawful act to the last extremity of the usurpation of power. The catena is complete. You commenced with a proclamation of war against the South. What have you done since? You have more than quintupled the army in disregard of the provinces of Congress. You have strangled the liberties of the people. You have caused the military arrest of citizens in jurisdictions where the Federal Courts have been in uninterrupted operation.

You have caused their house to be searched, and blank warrants to be distributed for inquisitions. You have suspended the writ of *habeas corpus.* You have administered to the army and civil officers of the Government a new and altered oath of allegiance. You have broken the sanctity of private correspondence, seizing the despatches preserved for years in the telegraph offices. You have violated the right of the people to keep and bear arms, robbed even the public authorities of arms in their possession, and of their purchase, and denied the right of a State, still remaining in the Union, to continue the privileges, which the Constitution has named and provided as "necessary to a free State." A State remaining in the Union is no longer free. A citizen remaining in the Union is no longer free: he is subject to arrest, by military process; to search, at pleasure; to espoinage, even in his private correspondence; to imprisonment, without recourse to the courts; to tests, whenever you choose to exact them; and to deprivation of arms, whenever your power may be thought to slacken, or your cowardice may happen to be shaken by alarms.

Such, sir, is but a hasty grouping of the acts

by which you have violated both the wisdom and the law of the Constitution, and erected a throne of despotism in your frightened capital. But the character of a despot is not completed by mere violations of law. There are violations of honor, morality and truth, more infamous than excesses of authority. It is of these, sir, that I would tell you as gloriously crowning you with a complete despotism—of these that I would remind the country, as staining you, beneath the gauds of the robe, with the very dregs of infamy.

The present stage of the war developes two facts which happening close together, at once expose and complete its policy. We see, first, the false tokens of your Government to the world: next, its betrayed pretences to its own citizens.

While, sir, your Government was attempting to amuse Europe with misrepresentations of the present war as a local mutiny, it was giving the lie to itself, and repeating it at every step in its own line of policy at home. You had assumed to establish, as against the South, a blockade, a severely belligerent and punitive right, at the same time that you protested against the recognition of the South as a belligerent. You insisted upon the denial to the South of a right that your own belligerent position towards her had called out. Not only this, you insisted upon the excision of the right of privateering from the South that your own Government had, in 1856, expressly reserved for the very occasion in which the South assumed to exercise it, namely, to supply the deficiency of a naval power.

You were caught, sir, in your own inconsistencies. It was not to be supposed that the very right your Government had laid the foundation for in its own position of belligerent, and that it had preserved, as a careful tradition of its own policy, was to be denied to the South by the world, only for the interest and benefit of your own Government. That, sir, would have been a degree of stultification and of subservience to your purposes, that you had no right to expect from the world. Your supreme commands at home, and the absolute fawning obedience of a lickspittle and hungry constituency have encouraged you to rather too high a dictation. Do not fret yourself, sir, with false expectations. Do not imagine that the world will surrender its conscience to you because Yankeedom has done it; that it will accept your falsehood and despotism, because "the Northern unit" thinks it truth and valor and honesty; and that it will listen unquestioningly to your maxims of public law, because "the great North" thinks and licks them over as sweet morsels of wisdom, and anoints them with the slime of its own grovelling passions.

Do not be illogical, sir. Do not mistake the sentiments of Illinois for the opinion of Europe. You have disgraced yourself and the great North enough already by the dancing and shuffling policy of your Premier towards the Governments of Europe.

Your blockade of the Southern coasts is already despised; it cannot be maintained. England and France are determined to have their cotton, tobacco and naval supplies from the seaports of the South. A line of such extent, with the numerous inlets on the coast from the James River to the Savannah, could, in the nature of things, by no application of the naval force at your command, be blockaded. Equally vain with the attempt to maintain a blockade, on such a line, constantly and vigilantly assailed by the whole commerce of Europe, will be your attempt, sir, to resist the public acknowledgment and exercise of the right of privateering on the part of the South —a right which was conceded to Greece in her revolt, and to the South American republics in their struggle for independence, and which, I repeat, was retained by your Government in express and permanent terms. The precedents of the Government at Washington will be turned against itself. "The militia of the seas" will destroy the commercial and navigating interests of the North; they will scour the South Pacific as well as other oceans of the world; they will penetrate into every sea, and will find as tempting prizes in the silk ships of China as in the gold-freighted steamers of California. The reversion upon your Government, sir, of its own maxims of public law is only needed to complete the ruin of the North, not only in her commercial interests, but in the immediate issues of the present war. The negation of the right of search will estop you from discovering contraband goods under the neutral flag of England or of France. It will leave the trade in contraband as free as any other. A moment's reflection will show you, sir, that the fixed precedents and cherished traditions of your own Government have only to be completely turned against itself by the world, to reduce it to the most miserable imbecility, and its people to their knees, and the deploring there of their own self-purchased destruction. The question alone remains, whether this complete reversion will be made;—and this question I am satisfied to leave to the justice and to the interest of the European Powers, when both these motives are conjoined and harmonized, to determine their action.

Heartily, sir, do I give thanks that the ambitious falsehood you sought to introduce into your foreign policy, on the subject of the present war, has not only been disappointed of its end, but has introduced a new element of controlling importance into this war. This element, which you have, unluckily for yourself, introduced, I believe to be almost vital and decisive. It will subordinate a controversy, which you hoped to keep in your own hands, and within the narrow restrictions of Mr. Seward's Yankee statesmanship, to the public law and the public opinion of the world. These are enduring, far-reaching, and ultimately decisive powers. Falseness and aggression, sir, in the war you are waging, can only be fatal to yourself. As abroad, the same policy has brought you into difficulties, so, at home, it will surround and destroy you. As the falsehood by which you sought to entrap the conscience and judgment of Europe has come back with retributive justice, so the falsehood of your policy at home will recoil and strike back upon yourself. The exposure of your policy to the world is sufficiently found in your intermeddling in Europe: it is seen at home, now, and in the light of day, in your *invasion of Virginia.*

This act, sir, has completed the infamy of your character. You have perpetrated it against all promises and pledges; you have multiplied by it falsehood on falsehood; you have put imagination on the rack to perceive what limit there can be fixed to your unscrupulousness, or what bounds set to a mendacious Government. Pretext has been exchanged for pretext, until the country, sir, has actually been bewildered at your enormous resources of falsehood. If, from all the slough of your proclamations, the mess of words you called an Inaugural, and the confused nonsense of your speeches, official and unofficial, one distinct proposition was drawn by the country, it was that you would not make an *aggressive* war upon the South. You defined for yourself the meaning of such a war, when, in your wayside speech at Indianapolis, you essayed a distinction between repossessing the forts, &c., in the South, and invading its territory, the latter of which only you esteemed to be war in its aggressive sense. Have you forgotten that distinction, sir? The country has only to look back upon it to discover your flagrant falsehood. Can you not cure it, sir, by some new distinction—some new pretext, so as to bring this invasion of Virginia under the terms of the Indianapolis speech, and the proclamations and manifestoes of a later date? Can't the adept Premier help you to a new logic, or a new falsehood?—or was he too plainly discovered in his ingenious ways by Judge Campbell, when the Judge, the equal of Mr. Seward in political position, twice charged him with "overreaching and equivocation," and he, the great representative man of the great North, twice slunk into silence under the charge?

Those, sir, who are committed to support you in all things, and to all extremities, are easily satisfied with explanations for every inconsistency or outrage you may choose to enact. Address yourself to these creatures, sir. You can, perhaps, explain to them that you have seized Alexandria to reclaim her as part of the District of Columbia; you can, perhaps, parade to them a pretext that you have been called into Virginia, "to protect Union men;" you may, perhaps, convince them that Alexandria is one of "the places" of the Government within the purview of the war proclamation; you may possibly even persuade the hang-mouthed listeners on your wisdom and bravery, that there is some old, strange claim of the Government to be revived to the odd-named Newsport-Newspoint at the mouth of the James River. As there are sometimes no limits to the mendacious utterances of a man, so, sometimes, there appear to be none to the servile acquiescence of fanatics and flatterers.

Virginia, and the honest world that regard her, sir, need not another word from you. Both understand you. You would repeat upon her your easy conquest of Maryland, seize her railroads, step by step, plant her with your troops, and then lay your strangling grasp upon her liberties. The falseness of policy, sir, superanimates the energy to oppose it. Your treachery has inspired all the vital forces of Virginia to compass your ruin, and directed all the scorn of the world to accomplish your infamy.

Filthy with falsehood, covered with treachery as with a garment, you will be, at once, expelled from Virginia, as by a sword of fire, and be driven from the honest conversations of the world, as a leprous despot, shunned and yet marked, hated and yet despised. The world, sir, has not yet outgrown the feelings which the inspired accounts of the first invader of man's kingdom of peace were intended to inspire. It is not likely to forget them—not likely to be unreminded of the old story of the Serpent, in the false words, subtle, gliding invasions, and anfractuous policy of Abraham Lincoln.

Without a word of premonition, against all promises and all expectations, in the night time, while the stars of the approaching morning alone watched in the sky, you glided into Virginia, silently and beautifully as a serpent in his slime and glittering scales. Let it be so! Let the serpent coil himself strongly! "The wisest of beasts," he is yet not the strongest. There are talons to fight him, to strip him, and to tear his writhing folds between heaven and earth, as his golden scales fall one by one in the sunshine, up which *the eagle* flies with his prey.

I am, &c.,

THE SOUTHERN SPY.

VIII.

LETTER TO THE REV. DR. TYNG OF NEW YORK.

BALTIMORE, 1861.

Dr. S. A. Tyng:

SIR: Your office admonishes me to address you respectfully. Be pleased, sir, however, to distinguish between the respect which I readily give to your office, and that which I must be studious to withhold from your person.

Sir, you are a minister of the gospel. May our Almighty Father in Heaven pardon me, if I say, in any other than the deepest humility and distrust, that I, too, am a member of His Church on earth, and a suppliant at the throne of His mercy.

Religion may have its military ideas, sir; they are ideas of necessity, not of wrath. It may be proper, it may be dutiful, though unwelcome, in a Christian man, sometimes to speak harshly, to chastise falsehood, and to let loose his wrath upon evil men. In connections with the secular press,

I may have spoken with severity. I claim the right to use it against bad men in high places, murdering my country or betraying it. But, sir, even the language of just denunciation, I would restrain against you, a priest of the church;— but, understand, sir, not that I esteem you less false or murderous than the politicians whom you serve, but because you are clothed in an office, holy and venerable in itself, however wretched and abandoned the man it may cover. The apostle was sorry to have denounced the whited Pharisee, who would have stopped his words with blows, because he "wot not that he was the high priest."

I will endeavor to write calmly; but I will not be satisfied to write less than truthfully.

Some time ago, sir, in making a hasty journey into the North, in which I was enabled to observe mutely, but narrowly, the sentiments and the signs of that section, there was put into my hands a New York paper of your own persuasion, containing a report of a Sunday sermon, delivered by you before the Bible Society, on the occasion of the presentation of Bibles to the troops enlisted for war upon the South. I will not foul my sheet with the name of this paper; and I deem it equally unnecessary, sir, to assoil it by the extended report of your extraordinarily vile remarks on this sabbatical occasion.

You were not satisfied to name my countrymen, and your "brethren" (to use the fondling term of the old poisoning hypocrisy of the North,) as "*pirates;*" you condemned them to a fate, at which demons only could rejoice; you consigned them to nameless horrors, and declared your belief that "*the Bible would singe and scald their polluted hands!*" There were Northern troops standing around you in the clamor and passion for blood. They cheered you, sir. You replied that "*they were worthy of the Bible:*" in the animation that their shouts inspired, you exclaimed, "how their names will glisten *in glory!*" You boasted of your own prowess in the work of death. You declared, in the bloody bravery and dialect of a murderer, that, as to the rebellious Southerners, "YOU *would shoot them down as mad dogs!*"

I shuddered to read such speeches, sir. But the horror of my feelings I cannot describe, as I continued to read what else fell from ministerial lips, poisoned with sickening shouts for blood. You spoke of the regiment of one "Billy Wilson," composed, as is notorious, of the thieves, costermongers, "fighting men" and murderers of New York. In rather strangely clerical phrase, and in a language which I had thought confined to the petting endearments of the Bowery, you referred to them as *"rare birds."* You spoke of their prowess. You, sir—you, an officer of God's church, to administer its comforts, and to teach its great mystery of salvation in fear and trembling, "*ventured* to say," that the *salvation* of these abandoned men might, probably, be obtained "by the consecration they had made of themselves!" In the report, there is an interpolation of "cheers" at the promise.

Great God, sir, is it possible that such awful, mocking, flippant, demon blasphemy should be uttered in the name of His church, and of His blessed Son, who "taketh away the sins of the world," and the utterer live on unconsumed by the Divine vengeance!

Sir, I promised you no words of denunciation. There can be none such for this.

By the way, sir, you took occasion to remark

to your wild auditors, that you had "served eighteen years of your ministry in Virginia." Is this really true? You will pardon me for questioning it, not only after the expressions of your desires for the drenching of this State in blood, but because, sir, of your total unlikeness, in every appearance, to all I have ever seen of the clergy in Virginia. Certainly, you have retained but little of the simplicity of the clerical manners of the South. You are known to be a "fashionable preacher," sir, over-fond of the sumptuousness and delicacies of your house, and of keeping great company around you. This class of clergy must have been extinguished in Virginia when you left it.

To shift further comments on your Bible-Society sermon, sir, and to avoid, for a moment, feelings which, while I dwell upon it, I must confess to be both indignant and distressful, I will tell you of a little experience of my own among the Episcopal clergy of the South.

..... In last winter, sir, on a rapid visit into a portion of the South, I passed one of the most wholesome and pleasant episodes of my life. On an occasion, which I need not particularize, I stopped at the house of an old and beloved dignitary of our church, whose piety, Christian scholarship and venerable years, are matters of fame and respect throughout the whole country. I had seen so much abroad, at least, of the fine living and ostentations of the superior ranks of the clergy, that when I approached the neighbourhood of this Nestorian diocesan of the Episcopal Church, I naturally amused myself with fancying the mode of my reception, in what I thought would be some splendid mansion filled with imposing displays of comforts and luxuries, and offering only a stiff and aristocratic welcome on the part of its lordly occupant. Never, sir, were delusions more entirely dispelled.

As I alighted at the porch of a farm-house, at once studiously plain and studiously tasteful, a bent figure, with white locks, came out to meet me. His eyes were the most gentle I ever recollect to have seen; there was a deep, clear peace in their expression, that at once subdued and charmed. His voice, as he bade me welcome, had the music of gentle and benevolent old age. The room into which I was conducted was both **parlor and study, and I looked in vain for one** evidence of luxury to mark the rank of the great scholar and Episcopalian. It was as bare, but as perfectly neat as the worn and carefully brushed suit of black in which he was clothed. The floor of the room was uncarpeted, though it was the depth of winter; the furniture was scanty, it would have been almost nothing on taking out the immense book cases that covered portions of the walls; a common deal chair, with a writing leaf, that the venerable man afterwards told me was a relic of his college days, was placed in the chimney-corner, and near it a large velvet-furred cat, evidently a pet, purred in the delight of the warm corner, and reached to the caresses of her master.

In this simple home I found the learned and evangelical Christian, whose name was venerated in all parts of the Union. The plainness and gentleness of his life won my instant esteem; and a religious conversation, inexpressibly sweet, completed the charms of his character.

My visit happened to be during the critical times of the sessions of the Peace Congress in Washington, when Virginia was exerting herself with the greatest power and urgency for the safety of the Union. Never shall I forget the friction and warmth of the feelings of my venerable host, as he dwelt upon the last existing hope of the maintenance of the Union. He paced the room in the excitement of his feelings. A noble flush would lighten up his aged features, as, at each pause in his walk, he would declare how "noble" it was in Virginia to strive as she was striving for the Union of our forefathers, and how "proud" he was of the Old Dominion in her Christian and national mission. He hoped and prayed for the preservation of the Union: he deplored the recklessness of the North in this respect; but not one word of enmity, or of temper, or even of exaggerated speech fell from his lips. Sir, you cannot wonder that I was struck by the example of such a life. When, long before daybreak, I prepared to set out to meet the train on the railroad, I found my venerable host already up before me, having built his own fire,—a custom, which, at nearly eighty, I learn, is still regular with him at dawn—and when I shook hands with him in the dark at the gate, with the flakes of a snow storm, which he quietly braved, scattering themselves over his venerable person,

I felt that I had parted with one of those extraordinary old Christian soldiers, clothed in the apostolic graces of all courage and all gentleness. Noble, beloved, venerable soldier of the Cross! Distressed, tossed and beaten about as my own life may be, I feel that I can ever look back upon that peaceful old man with an inspiration of love and prayer for his long continuance in the sweet conversations of his life, and in the dear service of Christ.

Many months had elapsed, sir, between this singular visit in the South and my perusal, on the waters of the Hudson, of your Sabbath oration on the war that had already broken out. I turned the pages of the New York paper in which I read it. On one of the pages I caught the title of some other religious remarks on the existing war. They bound me with their beauty; they expressed and breathed a Christian charity, that I had yet found in no treatment by laity or clergy of the unhappy war; they insisted upon the stern and unwelcome duty of the writer's State, cast out of the Union, as it were, to resist, with Christian manliness, the war thrust upon her; but they called yet for every limit of forbearance, they invoked charity, they expressed all abhorrence of blood, they plead the charities as well as the duties of the terrible emergency. I hastened to find the signature to these at once courageous and gentle remarks, uttered so evidently in the moving and tender spirit of our holy religion. It was the name of the venerable host, who had so welcomed me, and taught me new examples of life. It was the diocesan report of the Right Rev. William Meade, Bishop of Virginia!

Sir, I will say no more. I will not wound you with the contrast. Promise only to read these noble remarks, to repeat them to the North: and then, confronting them with your own words of bloody zeal, the two may stand, the two *must* stand to be judged not only in the sober second judgment of men, but in the sight of God, "not in the words which man's wisdom teacheth."

With respect for "the priest,"

THE SOUTHERN SPY.

IX.

LETTER TO GENERAL SCOTT.

MARYLAND, JULY 3, 1861.

Lt. Gen'l Winfield Scott, &c., &c., &c.

SIR: Some persons who depreciate your greatness, declare that your vanity is so excessive that it even rejects the sympathy of your friends. I allow myself to doubt this; and I refuse, sir, to pass by your misfortunes without condoling with them.

It is, indeed, a shame that you, sir, "an old soldier," and, as your admirers so justly say, one of the greatest Captains of the age, should be subjected to the infamous doubts of Northern papers, as to your military prowess, and even to egging annoyances of the Cabinet, because you have delayed to start on your triumphal career to Richmond. Who, sir, is the intermeddler in the Cabinet that will insist upon prying into and annoying your plans of military wisdom? Is it the pragmatical spirit of Montgomery Blair that gives you this annoyance—or the curiosity of "the little woman" from Illinois? Speak out, sir. Let the people know who dares to question or confront the wisdom of him, "who has passed his whole life in the service of his country."

Do not allow the Northern papers to wound your vanity. Do, sir, as many great men have had to do—console yourself with your own reflections of your greatness. If you have not yet "shelled" Richmond, or overrun Virginia, or captured "Mr." Jefferson Davis—whose life, by the way, you might have taken once, had it not been for your unfortunate "wounds" from a fall down stairs, which prevented you from accepting the risks of the *duello*—why has the country been so unjust as to have forgotten that you have, at last, assuaged Mr. Lincoln's personal fears, and gained a victory in the "moral results" of every conflict that has yet happened! And what deeds have you not enacted on your sofa in Washington, despite the pangs of the gout—what brilliant strategies have you not pointed out with the long reed with which you have reached from your sick couch to your military maps—and what important assurances have you not sent, from day to day, to the White House, that "nobody was hurt!"

The North, sir,—and even Mr. Montgomery Blair, are ungenerous only because they are ignorant. They do not know your plans; they mistook them for the easy and cheap expedient of marching to Richmond, and planting the Stars and Stripes in Capitol Square. You have disdained such easy victories: you have matured a more brilliant plan, and the country only depreciates it, because it does not know it.

Do you not recollect, sir, when a mutual friend in your private room lately urged to you to disclose your plans to him, what you said to him in reply. He asked how you proposed to subdue "the rebels." With knit brows, you opened your wide hand, and slowly and tightly closed it. The emphatic and eloquent reply needed no words. You proposed, with one broad grasp, to crush and strangle the miserable traitors. How grand such a plot of warfare—how much better than an easy march to Richmond—how worthy of the applause of the North, if it had only imagined the existence in your mind of a plan so comprehensive, so brilliant, and so satisfactory!

Sir, you have concealed your wisdom. The North has misapprehended you, the Cabinet have not been taken into your confidence; and they have censured you, only through mistake. Retrieve, sir, your misfortunes; afford to the North, and to the Government, an opportunity to recall their misjudgments, and to ascribe to you the hosannas of their praise. You will soon have the one hundred and eighty thousand troops in Virginia in your tightened and deadly grasp. You will easily strangle them all. The North has only to be patient, and you, sir, can still afford to be insolent to the Government, and asperous, as ever, to all vulgar inquisitors.

I am, &c.,

THE SOUTHERN SPY.

X.

LETTER TO EDWARD EVERETT.

MARYLAND, JULY ...., 1861.

To Mr. Edward Everett:

SIR: There are several kinds of falsehood. There is the open and direct falsehood; it is known in vulgar society as *the lie*, and is applied generally to men who are coarse and unartificial in their statements. Then there is the genteeler falsehood by implication; it is called by milder terms than the lie, only because it lacks its vulgar simplicity. Lastly, sir, there is still a more finished and educated kind of falsehood, that assumes the appearance of truth, and that sometimes uses the most elegant arts and the highest polish to engage belief. I will not denominate the order of this last kind of falsehood. How well I might be able to illustrate it in comments on the terse expression that he who "lies like truth most truly lies"—for decent reasons, believe me, sir—I forbear to essay. I am not fond of vulgarities; I, generally, discard them from my lexicon; and I certainly shall endeavour, sir, not to wound your fine taste by inelegant words.

Permit me, sir, rather to share in your own fastidious elegances of style; and in declining credence to the statements of your lately published letter on the war, addressed to a gentleman of Virginia, to testify how much it reads "like truth," and with what art and polish it is arranged. With this commencement, sir, which you are, no doubt, too much accustomed to flattery to value as highly as is intended, permit me to proceed to dissent from some of the views of your letter referred to.

It is not strange, sir, that you should begin the statements of your letter with a compliment to yourself. This is sometimes a common habit of great men. You assert that, until recently, you "sustained the South at the almost total sacrifice of influence and favor at home." I am not aware that this fact is as generally known as you presume it to be. What have *you* done for the South? I ask for information, sir. Of course, I am not disposed "to argue myself unknown;" I am not ignorant of you, sir. I know that you wrote and recited over the country a very flowery oration on the *pater patriæ;*—I hear that your eloquence never fails of feminine admiration;—I am apprised that you are a Latin and Greek scholar, acquainted with many of the modern tongues, and famous for the elegance of your language;—I have seen it abundantly advertised that you "wrote for the New York Ledger,"—I have read the celebrated classic letter which you signed, offering the tenderest sympathy to Senator Sumner for his chastisement in the Senate at the hands of a Southerner, whom you eloquently denominated as *brute* and *assassin;*—I am told that you have made innumerable Fourth-of-July speeches ; that you are a great orator, that you can commit the longest speeches to memory, that you have all the rules and artifices of eloquence at your fingers ends;—and I am even reminded of your matchless trick of eloquence in having once bribed a waiter, at a dinner at Faneuil Hall, to leave a small miniature flag sticking in a pyramid cake by your plate, that in the speech expected from you, you might take it up by a sort of dramatic surprise, and hold it aloft to match your peroration in an apostrophe to the Stars and Stripes. Pardon me, sir, for mentioning so small a circumstance. Even small things are interesting of the great. You cared for the flag only to match a figure of speech in your oration;—and even beyond this petty episode of a patriotic dinner, let me beg you, sir, to take care that you have not given more important hints, that, as a literary man of too much artifice, you have been fond of employing the sentiments and symbols of patriotism as mere dramatic elements, with no feeling higher or worthier in their use than that of heightening your eloquence, or adding to the graces of your composition.

I will not return to question what you have done for the South. Grant, sir, that you have done wonders to "sustain" her. You say that you have done so "at the almost total sacrifice of influence and favor at home." Unfortunately, in this expression, sir, you are too intent upon praising yourself to apprehend the conclusion it implies. This conclusion can only be, that the Northern people have been "almost totally" opposed to the rights of the South, and that those who have sustained them have done so at the loss of "influence and favor." This is an important confession, and as logical as it is important. I would not hurt your vanity, sir, especially after you had helped me to so important a fact. But could the South, sir, think it sufficient to repair the confession you make of the general hostility of the North towards her, that *you* sustained her! How, too, sir, does this confession consist with the after-declaration of your letter that the South was fully protected in the Union? Were *you*, sir, the North—were *you* to give that protection, without "influence and favor at home" —were *you* to assure the sustaining of her by the recitation of the Washington oration, or the aid of *Ledger* literature, or the resources of new and even more dramatic inventions of rhetoric? I will not deny that you are a great man, sir; I am only constrained to suggest that you too greatly value your services.

I pass to the statement next in order in the studied composition of your letter. You assert that you were well aware, partly from facts "within your *personal knowledge*," of the existence of a conspiracy of thirty years standing, among Southern politicians, to rupture the Union; and you add, that "the slavery question was but a *pretext* for keeping up agitation and rallying the South!"

This, sir, is too serious a matter of news to be treated by me in any other than the most serious style. Is it possible, sir, that you have so long been guilty of the misprision of the treason of this conspiracy, or of that part of it within your personal knowledge, divulging so grave and treasonable news neither to the Government nor to the country! You have criminally concealed facts that you profess made you acquainted with the inceptive steps of the conspiracy in the South that you now believe Mr. Lincoln to be right in scourging as "rebellion." How far removed is such conduct, sir, from "treason," in view of the Northern definitions of that term, and the late seizure of telegraphic dispatches to discover men as traitors, who knew of the conspiracy, with which you now boast an early personal acquaintance?

But there is still another, even more painfully glaring inconsistency in your statement quoted above. This statement follows just after your boast of sustaining the South, and in it, you style the slavery question but a *pretext* for agitating and rallying its people. If you did sustain the South, sir, I do not conceal my gratification at this circumstance;—but, however I might delight in observing Northern men standing up in defence of the rights and guarantied institutions of the South, I would certainly be sorry to see any one of them sustaining a people on an issue, which he might hereafter confess to be a pretext, or giving his support to any cause at the expense of honesty.

Briefly, sir, on the confessions of your own statement, did you act patriotically, according to your present standard of patriotism, in so long concealing your "personal knowledge" of the Southern conspiracy:—or did you act any more honestly in sustaining the South when you were convinced that the question of protecting her institutions was but a pretext, and a mere element to vitalize her conspiracy against the Union? It would be a needless and harsh gratuity for me, sir, to answer these questions. It might betray me into an offensive plainness of style, that might be thought vulgar, in its applications to a highly educated conscience like your own. You, certainly, have the fastidiousness of language to give nicer answers to such questions than a plain man too much accustomed to call things by their right names.

I pass, sir, to that portion of your letter more particularly applicable to the present emergencies, and which is, in fact, the gist of your communication. You admit that, up to the time of the possession of Fort Sumter by South Carolina, it was your opinion that if the seceded States were "determined to separate, *we had better part in peace.*" You cannot do less, sir, than make the admission of this your former opinion; you had busied yourself too much in notifying it to the country, to deny or to conceal it now. You are left to hunt a pretext for the very sudden conversion of your policy of peace to your present stimulations of a coercive war, and you pretend to find it in the old and worn excuse of the attack on Sumter. In one sense, the excuse is merely ridiculous. But it covers too deep a meaning to be dismissed so lightly. Whenever men are found making excuses for changes of opinion, irrational and opposite to facts, you may depend upon it, sir, that they are rather seeking to save their hypocrisy from too great an exposure than to enlighten their motives to others. The Sumter affair has afforded to thousands, in the North, a most flimsy and false excuse for loosing passions of hate against the South that had all along been festering in the concealments of their hearts. That event suddenly convinced them that the South was really resolved to separate; it disconcerted their hopes and plans of seducing her back into the Union by false and temporizing speeches; it utterly disappointed the Northern expectation that the South was not really in earnest, and that "all would come out right" by a little hypocrisy and affectation on the Nothern side; it snapped as a rotten net, their vile and cheap schemes of getting the South back into the Union by art and deceit; and men, finding no longer any purpose for concealment, threw aside their former professions, quickly determined to coerce what they could not cozen. This, sir, is the whole explanation of the Northern "reaction" at the occurrence at Sumter.

But permit me to examine a little closely what you say of this moving event. I give you, sir, the benefit of a full quotation, with italics of my own.

It was my opinion that, if they [the Cotton States] would abstain from further aggression, and *were determined to separate, we had better part in peace.* But the wanton attack on Fort Sumter (which took place, not from any *military necessity*, for what harm was a single company, cooped up in Charleston harbor, able to do to South Carolina? but for the avowed purpose of "stirring the blood" of the South, and thus bringing in the Border States), and the subsequent proceedings at Montgomery, have wholly changed the state of affairs. The South has *levied an unprovoked war* against the Government of the United States, the mildest and most beneficent in the world, and has made it the duty of every good citizen to rally to its support.

The excuse of the Sumter attack has served other parties beside yourself, sir, as a convenient handle for hypocrisy and falseness. To be used as such, of course, it has to be put into a convenient shape of words. You speak of it as "a wanton attack." How wanton on the part of the South—how, even, evitable on her part, when the Administration made the direct challenge, which the South had forewarned the Government at Washington that it would be constrained to accept? This is a simple question, sir; but it presents, I am persuaded, the whole issue of the Sumpter complication, and severely indicates where the responsibility for the collision lies.

There is a very wretched argument in your

statement above, which, wretched as it is, permit me to reverse against yourself. You say that there was no "military necessity" for the possession of the fort by South Carolina, as it was able to do her no harm. Then pray, sir, in what respect greater was the military necessity for the Government to retain it, if it was so powerless to control or to affect the seceded State?

It was no question of military necessity. The Government at Washington wanted the fort as an appanage of its sovereignty. So did South Carolina. And its possession by the latter, sir, was but the incident of the separation you say you had recommended! It was but the logical and legitimate conclusion of your own policy! Why should you complain that South Carolina should be in possession—and even bloodless possession—of the fort, which very fact is but the essential and inevitable carrying out of your own early recommendation of her separate sovereignty!

I am sorry, sir, that you are so poor a logician. Is it possible that a letter, containing such rubbish as the above, was, as the editors excused it, "written without thought of its publication" (although it is a little remarkable that the copy of a private letter, written to a gentleman in Virginia, should find its way back, through all the interruptions of the mails, to a paper in Boston.) Excuses may be readily made for weak fallacies in a literary man, or even in a contributor to "Bonner's Ledger," who affects a logical style. I give you the benefit of such excuses. But can there be any, sir, for wilful and open misstatements of facts?

I had hoped to discover no such undisguised committals in your letter, satisfied, when I commenced to read the opening of it, that there would be no falsehoods in it that would not be polished by your scholarship, or covered by the elegant arts of your style. I am disappointed in one paragraph. There, unfortunately, sir, you have descended to that vulgar openness and directness which I had occasion to condemn at the commencement of this letter. You have amused yourself by making one single paragraph a clot of falsehoods.

You say that "the accredited leaders of the Republican party, including the President-elect, uniformly *pledged themselves* to that effect," namely, "*to remove all sincere alarm, on the part of the South, that their constitutional rights were threatened.*" You add, "that the two houses, by a constitutional majority, pledged themselves, in like manner, against any future amendment of the constitution *violating the rights of the South.*" When, sir, did Abraham Lincoln ever give such pledges? What more did the two Houses of Congress do than to declare in favor of an amendment that only re-affirmed the Constitution not to abolish slavery *in the States*, which had the opposition of sixty Republicans in the House of Representatives? To call such gratuitous legislation as this concession and security to the South, is but to add insult and wantonness to misrepresentation.

There is one excuse, sir, which you make for the conversion of your former position looking towards peace, to your present warlike attitude that is so entirely personal, that I shall treat it with becoming brevity. You say, "when General Beauregard proceeds to execute his threat, his red hot cannon balls and shells will not spare the roof that shelters my daughter and four little children at Washington, nor my own roof in Boston. Must I, because I have been the steady friend of the South, sit still, while he is battering my house about my ears?"

Your excuse, sir, seems to be faithfully copied from Abraham Lincoln's anxious pleas for the safety of his person. Do not be alarmed, sir. Nerve yourself to resist the magnetic influences of the royal fears of President Lincoln. Recommend your friends to do the same, before the whole North is shaking in unison with the daily tremblings of the occupant of the White House. The terrible General Beauregard, "*with his red hot cannon balls and shells,*" will scarcely harm you, especially as you have engaged his mercy in advance, by attesting in the same breath, in which you exclaim your fears of him, what a "steady" friend you have been of the South! I congratulate you on so early supplications for safety. I would assure your fears, sir. But, really, so strongly are they expressed, that in concluding this letter, I must confess to be in doubt, sir, whether I shall leave you to suffer more from the disorders of your conscience, or the visions which distress you of the dreadful Beauregard, with his "red hot" implements of war.

In ending these lines, it is due to make one explanation. The task of a writer is petty and unworthy to answer arguments so vapid as those just passed in review. Understand then, sir, that I have noticed your letter only because it was the production of a man holding a certain public position that was, in itself, not beneath notice. Permit me thus to dismiss you. Your public position is not important enough to warrant any further correspondence.

I am, &c.,

THE SOUTHERN SPY.

THE BOOK FOR THE TIMES.
BLACK DIAMONDS.

[*Second Edition.*]

Characterized, by the leading presses of the country, as *the best book* ever published on the Society of the South. Read the notices of the press.

"SLAVE LIFE IN THE SOUTH."*

In general we are strongly averse to mixing up special questions in ethics, or in politics, with what is called polite literature. Artistically viewed, we doubt whether the mixture is ever allowable. Even satiric poetry we take it, forms no exception to the rule ; for it is the province of that species of literature to attack wickedness and folly from the standpoint of admitted maxims of morality and wisdom, not to agitate debatable or unsettled problems. The introduction into the novel or poem of subjects pertaining to strict polemics, or to severe philosophy, as the main purpose of the work, produces an incongruous association, which is never agreeable and is often disgusting. Who wants to read a novel designed to illustrate the beauties of free trade or a protective tariff? Who *does* read Montgomery's maudlin poem, or Longfellow's sentimental cant in rhyme, on the awful sin of negro slavery?

* From the *New Orleans Delta*, Editorial.

Since t'e publication of Mrs. Stowe's "Uncle Tom's Cabin," which led the van of a frightful procession of books of a similar order on both sides of the slavery question, every reader of experience, taste, and discrimination, is predisposed to turn with loathing from any issue from the press whose title page has a perceptible squinting toward the vexed and vexatious subject. He is inclined to avoid it as a premeditated bore and deliberate swindle—a delusion and a snare—a cunning "dodge," by which he may be made the victim of self-inflicted twaddle. Of course there is frequently much matter of pith and moment in the numerous books in which the discussion of the slavery question, in all, or a few of its aspects, is thrown into the shape of stories or sketches. Indeed, there are some that touch the subject in a way so incidental and natural, and with so little of a partisan or disputatious spirit, that if the predisposition against them be once overcome, they may be read with equal entertainment and instruction.

Among the last productions to which we allude, we unhesitatingly place a small and unpretending volume, being a series of short sketches of slave life in the South, in the form of letters originally addressed by the author, Edward A. Pollard, of Washington City, to his friend, David M. Clarkson, of Newburgh, New-York.

The author appears to be a thorough Southernor in education, opinion, sympathy, and attachment; yet, his letters are *remarkably free from sectional prejudice and acerbity,* and, in truth, contain sketches that are amongst the *most Catholic, and tolerant, and genial,* we ever had occasion to peruse. He would seem to have traveled much, to have observed much, and to know much of various countries and peoples. But the negro nature he especially knows, profoundly, intimately; knows it, not by intellection merely, but also by heart; knows it, not through the cold light of ethnological science only, but most of all, through the warm, enkindling recollections of boyhood and youth. The negro, who, in his true nature, is always a boy, let him be ever so old, is better understood by a boy, than by a whole academy of philosophers, unless the boy element in the said philosophers is unusually long-lived and prosperous. The author, in this case, guided by his boy-knowledge of the negro, cannot misconceive or untruthfully delineate him. How appreciative, how loving, how tender and sympathetic he is in his delineations, we will let a few extracts show.

* * * * *

From the New-York News.

Mr. Pollard, of Virginia, is a Southern gentleman of the true stamp. He knows human nature well. . . . . We can promise all an ample reward for the cost and trouble of an acquaintance with the contents of this most interesting book. The letters are so many jewels in their way —black by the subject, but brilliantly lightsome in it. It is a little mine full of promised diamonds. Go and dig deep within its limits and be satisfied.

From De Bow's Review.

It abounds in incidents of Southern slaves and masters, illustrating, very happily, the patriarchal relation which subsists between the races of the South, and defending the institution more than all argument, from the assaults of ignorance or prejudice.

From the Mobile Register.

They are, beyond doubt, the most life-like delineations of the negro ever drawn with the pen. The work is original in its conception, and on its first publication, in the form of detached letters to a Northern friend, attracted no little attention, and must have effected much good in free labor regions. It will be read with interest at the South also, and we trust that our section will not forever deserve the reproach of despising its own literary talent, and discouraging the treatment of the subjects which concern it most.

From the Lynchburg Virginian.

Mr. Pollard describes the negro—his habits, his affections, his religion, his aspirations—not from hearsay, as do most writers, but from actual observation of, and association with him. Reared in Virginia, he displays that knowledge of negro character which can only be gained from seeing him in his appropriate sphere—a laborer upon a Southern plantation. It is the best portrait of the Southern slave we have ever seen drawn.

A BRILLIANT AND SPLENDID SOUTHERN BOOK.
In Press and will be ready Dec. 10th.

CAUSE and CONTRAST; *an Essay on the American Crisis.* By T. W. MacMahon.

Which we will publish in a few days. We do not hesitate to aver—for it has been so pronounced by competent and distinguished critics—that this is among the most comprehensive, brilliant, scholarly, charming, able and conclusive books that has yet appeared in exposition of Southern political philosophy. Its matter is erudite and profound, and the style in which i is composed is rarely rivalled. While blending the earliest transactions of men with those of the present, it is as fascinating as any novel—a work truly suitable for both sexes; for the student and the people. In amplitude of illustration it is rich, classical and elegant; and its logic is invincible.

The following are commendations by gentlemen who read portions of the manuscript:

From the Richmond Whig.

"It discusses, with rare ability and learning, the institution of slavery in all its aspects, as well as the social and political distinctions between the people of the Confederate States and those of the U. S. The style is ornate, glowing and eloquent. We predict that it will produce a sensation; take its place among standard literature; and have the effect of banishing from our midst the hurtful offspring of the morbid and prolific press of the North."

From the Dispatch.

"We have read portions of the MSS., and we pronounce it beautiful, excellent, and conclusive. We hope that it will obtain the circulation that it merits, not only in America, but in Europe."

We might continue similar extracts from the *Examiner,* Charleston *Mercury,* and o her journals, if space permitted. The work will be ready in a few days; one octavo volume, pica type, and published at ONE DOLLAR, with the usual discount to the trade.

Orders, to receive prompt attention, should be addressed to
WEST & JOHNSTON, *Publishers,*
145 Main street, Richmond, Va.

www.ingramcontent.com/pod-product-compliance
Lightning Source LLC
Chambersburg PA
CBHW020146170426
43199CB00010B/913